Contents

How to use this book

Each page has a title telling you what it is about.

Instructions look like this. Always read these carefully before starting.

This shows you how to set out your work. The first question is done for you.

Read these word problems very carefully. Decide how you will work out the answers.

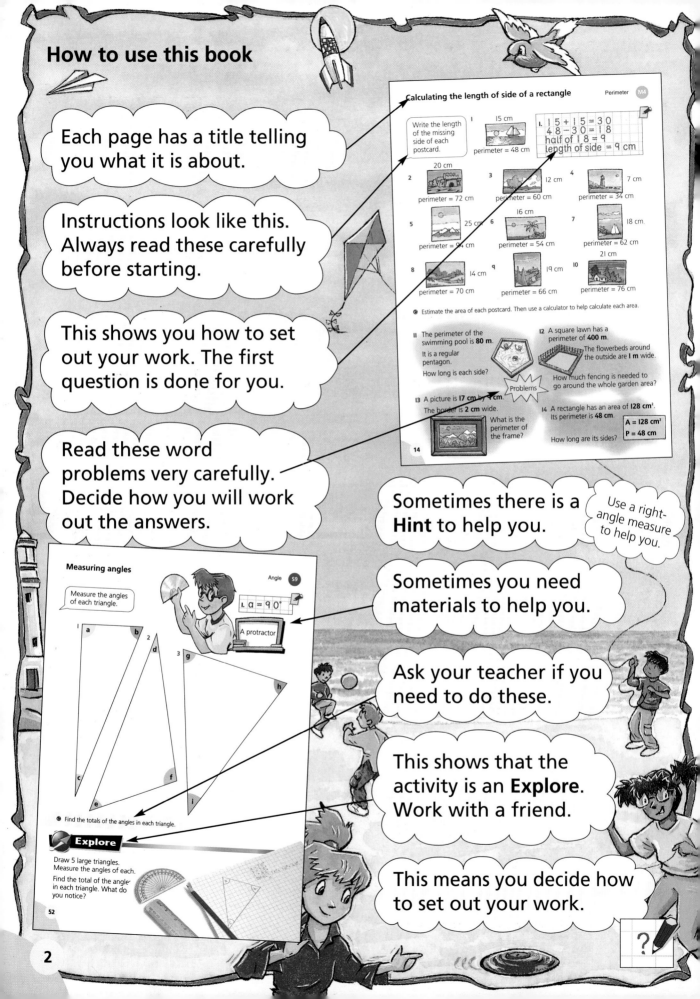

Calculating the length of side of a rectangle
Perimeter M4

Write the length of the missing side of each postcard.

1. $15 + 15 = 30$
$48 - 30 = 18$
half of $18 = 9$
length of side $= 9$ cm

1 15 cm perimeter = 48 cm

2 20 cm perimeter = 72 cm

3 12 cm perimeter = 60 cm

4 7 cm perimeter = 34 cm

5 25 cm perimeter = 94 cm

6 16 cm perimeter = 54 cm

7 18 cm. perimeter = 62 cm

8 14 cm perimeter = 70 cm

9 19 cm perimeter = 66 cm

10 21 cm perimeter = 76 cm

Estimate the area of each postcard. Then use a calculator to help calculate each area.

Problems

11 The perimeter of the swimming pool is **80 m**. It is a regular pentagon. How long is each side?

12 A square lawn has a perimeter of **400 m**. The flowerbeds around the outside are **1 m** wide. How much fencing is needed to go around the whole garden area?

13 A picture is **17 cm** by **9 cm**. The border is **2 cm** wide. What is the perimeter of the frame?

14 A rectangle has an area of **128 cm²**. Its perimeter is **48 cm**. How long are its sides?
A = 128 cm²
P = 48 cm

14

Sometimes there is a **Hint** to help you.

Use a right-angle measure to help you.

Sometimes you need materials to help you.

Measuring angles
Angle S9

Measure the angles of each triangle.

1. $a = 90°$

A protractor

Find the totals of the angles in each triangle.

Explore

Draw 5 large triangles. Measure the angles of each. Find the total of the angles in each triangle. What do you notice?

52

Ask your teacher if you need to do these.

This shows that the activity is an **Explore**. Work with a friend.

This means you decide how to set out your work.

?

Millimetres, centimetres, metres and kilometres

Write the missing numbers.

1   m = 100 cm

 I. 1 m = 1 0 0 cm

2 1 cm = mm

3 50 mm = cm

4   m = 1400 cm

5 20 cm =  mm

6   mm = $\frac{1}{2}$ cm

7 200 cm = m

8 $\frac{1}{4}$ m =  cm

9 100 mm =  cm

10 12 m =  cm

11  m = 1000 mm

12 10 m = cm

13  m = 2000 cm

14  cm = 20 mm

15 2.5 m = mm

16  m = 3000 cm

---

Write each distance in metres.

17

17. 1·5 km = 1 5 0 0 m

18   2·5 km

19   0·5 km

20   1·25 km

1·5 km

21   3·5 km

22   2·25 km

23   1·75 km

e Write each distance in centimetres and millimetres.

3

Millimetres, centimetres, metres and kilometres

Length M1

Write how far each has gone in metres.

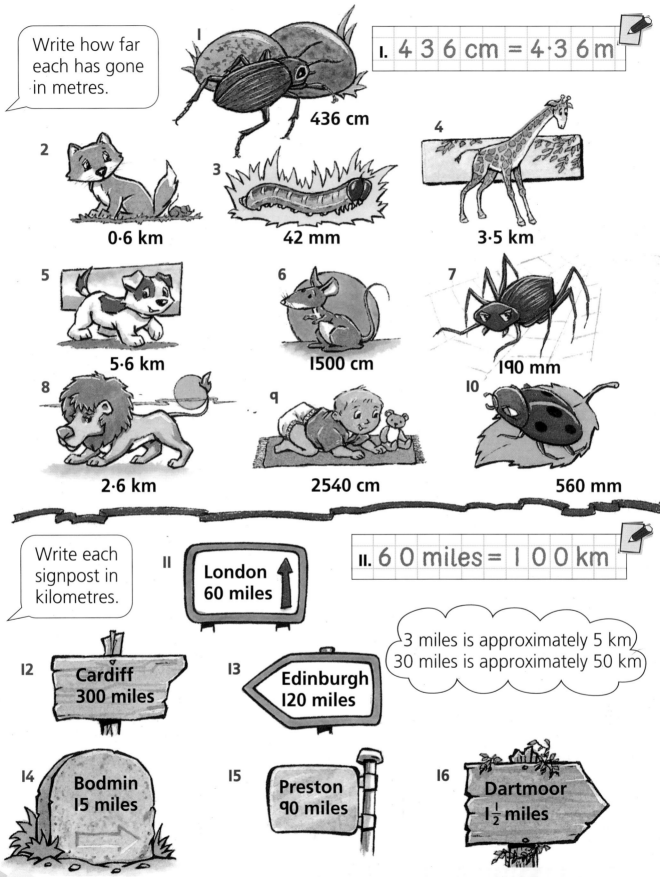

I. 4 3 6 cm = 4·3 6 m

1. 436 cm

2. 0·6 km

3. 42 mm

4. 3·5 km

5. 5·6 km

6. 1500 cm

7. 190 mm

8. 2·6 km

9. 2540 cm

10. 560 mm

Write each signpost in kilometres.

11. London 60 miles

II. 6 0 miles = 1 0 0 km

3 miles is approximately 5 km
30 miles is approximately 50 km

12. Cardiff 300 miles

13. Edinburgh 120 miles

14. Bodmin 15 miles

15. Preston 90 miles

16. Dartmoor $1\frac{1}{2}$ miles

e Write each distance in metres.

Measuring in centimetres and millimetres

Measure each line. | Write the lengths in centimetres.

 a. 3·7 cm

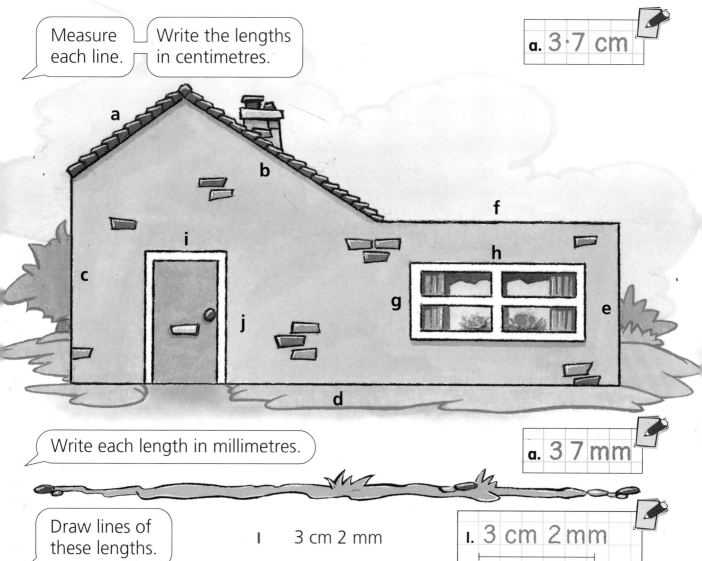

Write each length in millimetres.

a. 3 7 mm

Draw lines of these lengths.

1   3 cm 2 mm

1. 3 cm 2 mm

2 4 cm 7 mm	**3** 2 cm 9 mm	**4** 5 cm 5 mm	**5** 1 cm 3 mm
6 3 cm 4 mm	**7** 4 cm 1 mm	**8** 3 cm 7 mm	**9** 6 cm 6 mm

Explore

Draw a picture using only straight lines.

Label each line with its length.

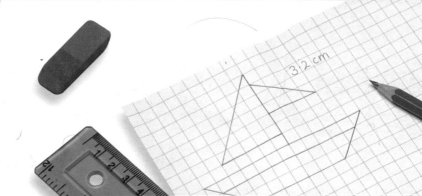

3.2 cm

Grams and kilograms

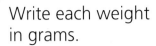

Write each weight in grams.

I. 1·42 kg

1. $1 \cdot 4 \; 2 \; k \; g = 1 \; 4 \; 2 \; 0 \; g$

2   0·75 kg

3   0·94 kg

4   1·33 kg

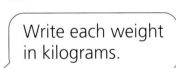

5   0·25 kg

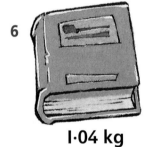

6   1·04 kg

7   0·86 kg

e   Write the weights in order.

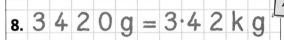

Write each weight in kilograms.

8   3420 g

8. $3 \; 4 \; 2 \; 0 \; g = 3 \cdot 4 \; 2 \; k \; g$

9   1240 g

10   3040 g

11   600 g

12   7500 g

13   9001 g

14   1250 g

Grams and kilograms

Write the missing numbers.

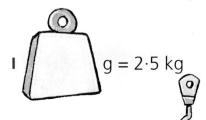

1 ▮ g = 2·5 kg

1. 2 5 0 0 g = 2·5 kg

2 ▮ g = 4·6 kg

3 346 g = 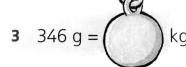 ▮ kg

4 ▮ g = $\frac{1}{2}$ kg

5 1750 g = ▮ kg

6 $\frac{1}{4}$ kg = ▮ g

7 3000 g = ▮ kg

8 2·33 kg = ▮ g

9 300 g = ▮ kg

10 0·75 kg = ▮ g

11 1$\frac{1}{2}$ kg = ▮ g

12 ▮ kg = 2550 g

13 ▮ g = 2$\frac{1}{4}$ kg

❷ Write the weights in kilograms in order.

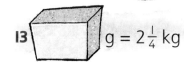

Find each object.

Write its weight in grams.

14
14. my shoe weighs 4 2 5 g

15

16

17

18

19

20
Paint

❷ Can you find an object that weighs approximately 325 g?

Estimating weight

> Choose the closest weight.

> Write each weight in kilograms.

I. $3500 \text{ g} = 3.5 \text{ kg}$

1

| 350 g | 3500 g | 35 000 g |

2

| 450 g | 4500 g | 45 000 g |

3

| 60 g | 600 g | 60 000 g |

4

| 9·9 g | 99 g | 990 g |

5

| 40 g | 400 g | 4000 g |

6

| 300 g | 3000 g | 30 000 g |

Problems

7 Selma is packing to go on holiday.

Her empty case weighs **2800 g**.

She packs her clothes which weigh **15 500 g**, then her CD player which weighs **950 g**.

She also takes her walking boots which weigh **4500 g**.

The baggage allowance is **25 kg**.

How much more can Selma pack?

Can she take her towel which weighs **800g**?

8 Tom is cooking.

His recipe is written in ounces. If **100 grams** is about **4 ounces**, write the recipe in grams.

Chocolate Biscuit Cake

4 ounces margarine
4 ounces sugar
4 ounces cocoa
3 ounces golden syrup
2 ounces raisins
8 ounces broken digestive biscuits

I. Melt the margarine.
2. Stir in the other ingredients.
3. Press the mixture into a tin.
4. Leave to cool.
5. Eat!

Area of rectangles

Write the area of each rectangle.

1

1. area = 2 × 6
        = 12 cm²

2

3

4

The squares are square centimetres.

5

6

7

Write the area of each rectangle.

8. area = 2 × 3 = 6 cm²

8

9

10

11

13

12

Length × breadth

Write the area of each rectangular field in square metres.

1. 90 m / 30 m

I. area = 90 × 30
   = 2700 m²

2. 80 m / 20 m

3. 45 m / 100 m

4. 60 m / 20 m

5. 70 m / 40 m

6. 120 m / 50 m

7. 60 m / 60 m

8. 100 m / 120 m

9. 110 m / 40 m

10. 90 m / 80 m

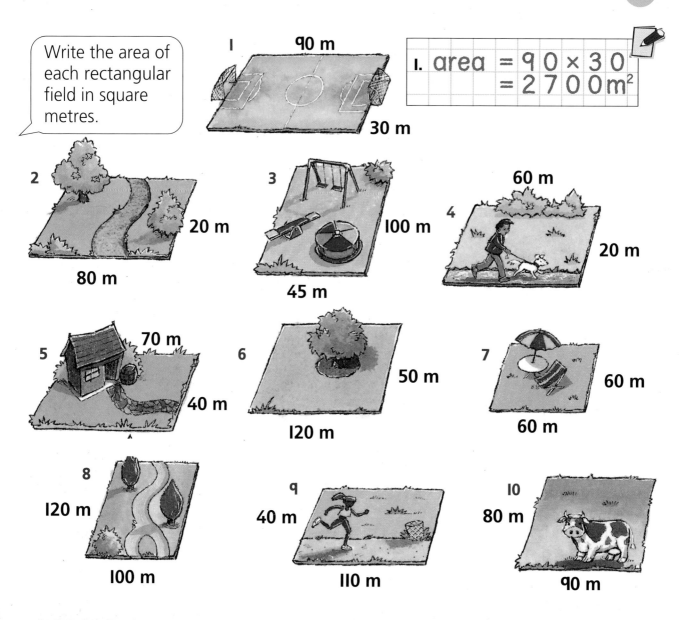

e Which has the larger area, a 120 m × 90 m field or a 110 m × 100 m field?

Explore

Four rectangular pictures each have an area of 2400 cm².

The sides are all multiples of 5.

What sizes could the pictures be?

A = 2400 cm²

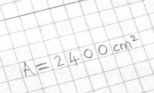

Calculating area

Copy each shape. — Divide it into 2 rectangles. — Write the total area.

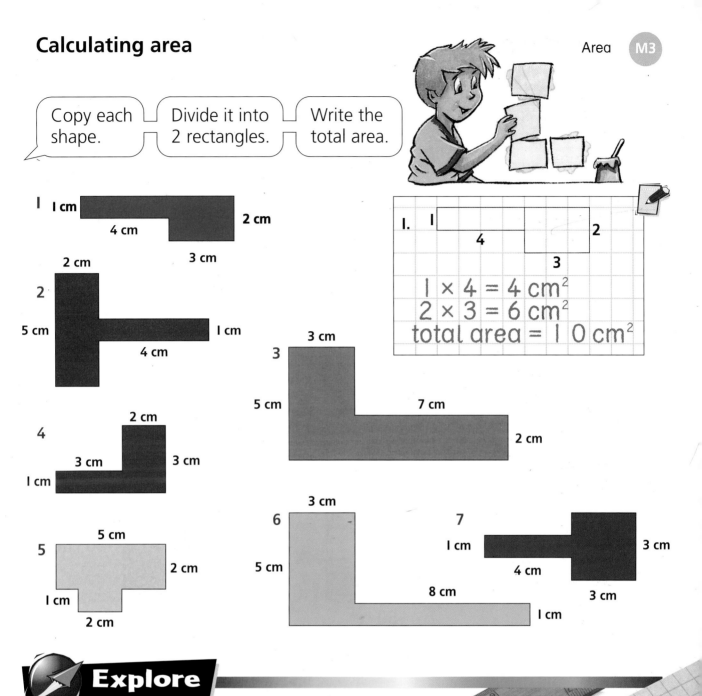

1.

$$1 \times 4 = 4 \text{ cm}^2$$
$$2 \times 3 = 6 \text{ cm}^2$$
$$\text{total area} = 10 \text{ cm}^2$$

1   1 cm   4 cm   2 cm   3 cm

2   2 cm   5 cm   4 cm   1 cm

3   3 cm   5 cm   7 cm   2 cm

4   2 cm   3 cm   3 cm   1 cm

5   5 cm   2 cm   1 cm   2 cm

6   3 cm   5 cm   8 cm   1 cm

7   1 cm   4 cm   3 cm   3 cm

Explore

Use centimetre squared paper.

Draw different L-shapes.

Find the area of each.

$$6 \times 2 = 12$$
$$3 \times 5 = 15$$
$$\text{area} = 27 \text{ cm}^2$$

Perimeter of rectangles

Write the perimeter of each picture.

I. perimeter = 5 0 + 3 0 + 5 0 + 3 0
= 1 0 0 + 6 0 = 1 6 0 cm

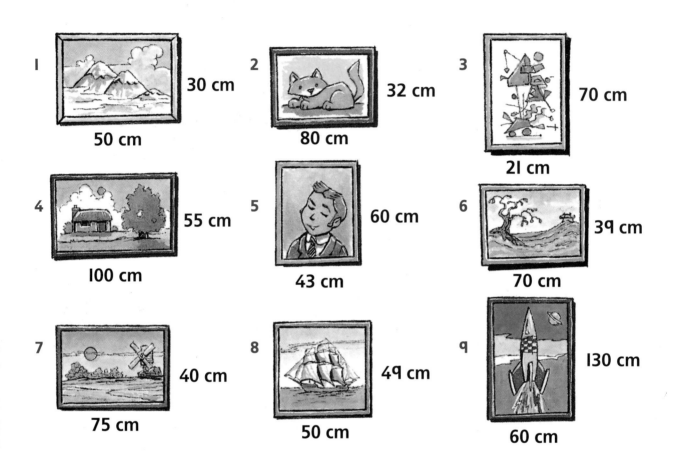

1 30 cm 50 cm

2 32 cm 80 cm

3 70 cm 21 cm

4 55 cm 100 cm

5 60 cm 43 cm

6 39 cm 70 cm

7 40 cm 75 cm

8 49 cm 50 cm

9 130 cm 60 cm

⊖ Write the area of each picture.

Draw each rectangle. Calculate its perimeter.

10 3 cm by 5 cm   11 4 cm by 2 cm

12 10 cm by 8 cm   13 13 cm by 3 cm

14 6 cm by 9 cm   15 7 cm by 11 cm

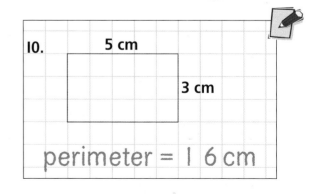

10.   5 cm

3 cm

perimeter = 1 6 cm

Perimeter of polygons

Write the perimeter of each regular polygon.

1

4 cm

1. perimeter = 6 × 4 cm
            = 24 cm

2

9 cm

3

12 cm

4

27 cm

5

2·5 cm

6

13·25 cm

7

7·1 cm

❷ Write the name of each polygon.

Write the perimeter of each shape.

8

6 cm

2 cm   2 cm

2 cm   2 cm

6 cm

8. 4 + 12 + 4 = 20
   perimeter = 20 cm

9

10 cm

11 cm   11 cm

20 cm   20 cm

11 cm   11 cm

25 cm

10

38 cm

15 cm   12 cm

15 cm   12 cm

38 cm

11

24 cm

24 cm

24 cm   24 cm

24 cm

24 cm

❷ Write the name of each shape.

Calculating the length of side of a rectangle

> Write the length of the missing side of each postcard.

1

15 cm

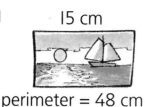

perimeter = 48 cm

```
1.  15 + 15 = 30
    48 – 30 = 18
    half of 18 = 9
    length of side = 9 cm
```

2

20 cm

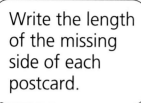

perimeter = 72 cm

3

12 cm

perimeter = 60 cm

4

7 cm

perimeter = 34 cm

5

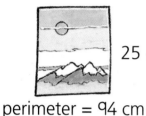

25 cm

perimeter = 94 cm

6

16 cm

perimeter = 54 cm

7

18 cm

perimeter = 62 cm

8

14 cm

perimeter = 70 cm

9

19 cm

perimeter = 66 cm

10

21 cm

perimeter = 76 cm

---

e Estimate the area of each postcard. Then use a calculator to help calculate each area.

11 The perimeter of the swimming pool is **80 m**.

It is a regular pentagon.

How long is each side?

Problems

12 A square lawn has a perimeter of **400 m**.

The flowerbeds around the outside are **1 m** wide.

How much fencing is needed to go around the whole garden area?

13 A picture is **17 cm** by **9 cm**.

The border is **2 cm** wide.

What is the perimeter of the frame?

14 A rectangle has an area of **128 cm²**.

Its perimeter is **48 cm**.

How long are its sides?

$$A = 128 \text{ cm}^2$$
$$P = 48 \text{ cm}$$

Litres and millilitres

Write how many litres.

1. **400 ml**

1. $400 \text{ ml} = 0.4 \text{ l}$

2. **4200 ml**

3. **2500 ml**

4. **450 ml**

5. **1100 ml**

6. **770 ml**

7. **2000 ml**

8. **4400 ml**

9. **9900 ml**

10. **1500 ml**

Write how many millilitres.

11. **0.05 l**

11. $0.05 \text{ l} = 50 \text{ ml}$

12. **1.5 l**

13. **5.25 l**

14. **2.5 l**

15. **0.25 l**

16. **6.006 l**

17. **9.9 l**

Choose the closest capacity. | Write it in litres.

I. 3 0 0 ml = 0·3 l

1

Shampoo

| 30 ml | 300 ml | 3000 ml |

2

| 2·5 ml | 25 ml | 250 ml |

3

| 10 ml | 100 ml | 1000 ml |

4

| 33 ml | 330 ml | 3300 ml |

5

Milk

| 15 ml | 150 ml | 1500 ml |

6

| 50 ml | 500 ml | 5000 ml |

7

| 300 ml | 3000 ml | 30 000 ml |

8

| 20 ml | 200 ml | 2000 ml |

9

| 100 ml | 10 000 ml | 100 000 ml |

 Explore

You have 4·99 l of juice and bottles of 3 different sizes.

Find the least number of bottles needed to hold all the juice. Each bottle must be full.

| 250 ml | 300 ml | 330 ml |

Capacity problems

Each milkshake uses a different amount of flavour powder.

Calculate the cost of making each milkshake.

$$1. \ 3 \times 5 \ ml = 15 \ ml$$
$$10 \ ml \ costs \ 20 \ p$$
$$5 \ ml \ costs \ 10 \ p$$
$$15 \ ml \ costs \ 30 \ p$$

1  **Raspberry**

10 ml costs 20p

2 **Chocolate**

10 ml costs 30p

Each teaspoon is 5 ml.

3  **Blackcurrant**

10 ml costs 40p

4  **Banana**

10 ml costs 25p

5 **Strawberry**

10 ml costs 30p

6  **Melon**

20 ml costs 50p

7 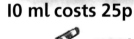 **Lime**

15 ml costs 30p

8  **Blueberry**

25 ml costs 50p

9 Dad's car uses **5 litres** of petrol for every **35 miles** driven.

Dad spends **£18** on petrol. It costs **90p** a litre.

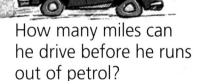

How many miles can he drive before he runs out of petrol?

Problems

10 Harvey the hairdresser buys **10 litres** of shampoo for **£45**.

He puts it in bottles holding **250 ml**. He sells each bottle for **£1·50**.

£1·50

How much profit does Harvey make?

Days, weeks, months and years

Write the number of days in each month.

1 January

I. January 31 days

Use your knuckles.

J F M A M J J A S O N D

2 August

3 March

4 October

5 February

6 September

7 June

8 April

9 May

10 December

11 July

12 November

Write how many days.

13 2 weeks

13. 2 weeks = 14 days

14 I week 4 days

15 the months without an 'r' in their names

16 I year

17 the years 2000 and 2001

18 February 2004

19 the last 6 months of the year

18

Write how many hours.

1 Monday and Tuesday

1. 2 days
   1 day = 2 4 hours
   2 days = 4 8 hours

2 Wednesday, Thursday and Friday

3 360 minutes

4 6000 minutes

5 1st to 10th February

6 3600 seconds

7 half a day

8 Sundays in March

9 April

10 one third of June

Write the length of each programme in seconds.

11 QUIZ FOR A MILLION

II. 2 0 minutes
    = 1 2 0 0 seconds

6:20 p.m. to 6:40 p.m.

12 WESTSIDERS

7:50 p.m. to 8:20 p.m.

13 NEWS

11:55 a.m. to 12:05 p.m.

14 BREAKFAST

7:30 a.m. to 8:10 a.m.

Choose units to measure each length of time.

1 London to Cardiff by train

i. hours and minutes

2 the time you can hold your breath

3 cleaning your teeth

4 making a cake

5 jumping 3 times

6 a cricket match

7 drinking a cup of tea

8 how long you sleep in your life

9 the time between seeing lightning and hearing thunder

10 school holidays

Each child reads 100 pages.

Write how long each takes.

ii. 2 pages in 1 minute
1 page in $\frac{1}{2}$ minute
$100 \times \frac{1}{2} = 50$
100 pages in 50 minutes

2 pages in 1 minute

1 page in 120 seconds

2 pages in 300 seconds

1 page in 90 seconds

Write these as 24-hour clock times.

1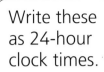

1. 4:30 p.m. → 16:30

4:30 p.m.

2

8:00 a.m.

3

1:15 p.m.

4

3:30 p.m.

5

8:25 a.m.

6

9:25 p.m.

7

9:00 a.m.

8

7:20 p.m.

9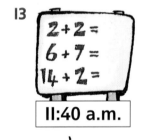

7:30 a.m.

10

10:35 a.m.

11

3:00 a.m.

12

5:50 p.m.

13

11:40 a.m.

Write each time as a.m. or p.m.

14

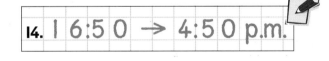

14. 16:50 → 4:50 p.m.

15
9:45

16
13:02

17
15:21

18
22:48

19
19:21

20
8:48

21
17:53

22
10:00

Wild West Adventure Park

Day Plan

Cowboy Corral	11:40	Rocking Rodeo	16:35
Spur Swinger	12:30	High Noon	17:05
Ranch Café	13:20	The Cattle Rustler	18:10
Thunder Mine	14:25	Stetson Splash	19:05
Runaway Train	15:50	Homeward Bound	20:15

Write these start times as a.m. or p.m.

1   Ranch Café

> 1. 13:20 → 1:20 p.m.

2   The Cattle Rustler   3   Cowboy Corral   4   Homeward Bound

5   Thunder Mine   6   Spur Swinger   7   High Noon

How long is spent at:

8   Rocking Rodeo

> 8. 16:35 → 17:05
> 30 minutes

9   The Cattle Rustler   10   Ranch Café   11   High Noon

12   Runaway Train   13   Cowboy Corral   14   Stetson Splash

Explore

Design your own theme park timetable.

Use 24-hour clock times.

Timetables

Each hockey match lasts 25 minutes. Write the finish times.

I. 1 4:0 0

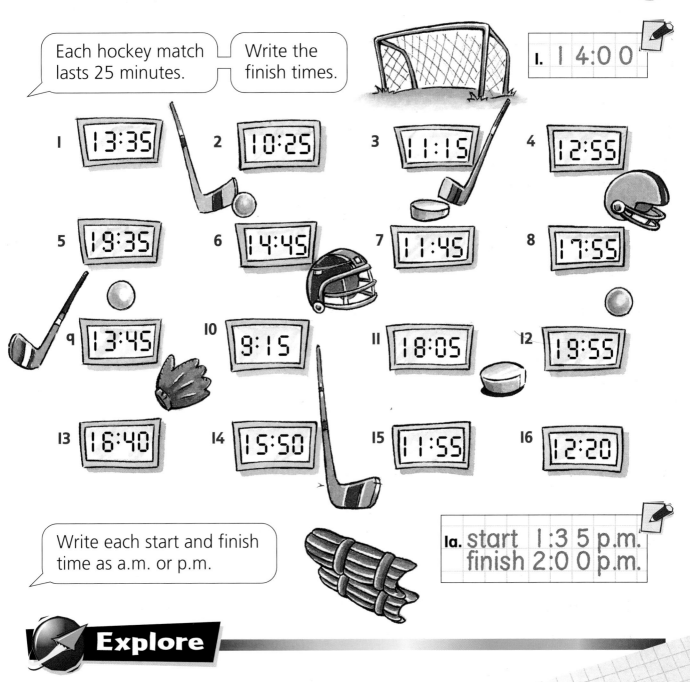

1 13:35

2 10:25

3 11:15

4 12:55

5 19:35

6 14:45

7 11:45

8 17:55

9 13:45

10 9:15

11 18:05

12 19:55

13 16:40

14 15:50

15 11:55

16 12:20

Write each start and finish time as a.m. or p.m.

Ia. start 1:3 5 p.m.
finish 2:0 0 p.m.

Explore

Write the timetable for a hockey tournament.

The first match starts at 14:00.

Each game is 25 minutes long.

Allow 10 minutes between each game.

Write the start and finish times for 10 games.

23

Write when each shop opens and closes as a.m. or p.m.

Write how long each shop stays open.

```
1. opens        1:05 p.m.
   closes      10:55 p.m.
   9 hours 50 minutes
```

1

Opens 13:05
Closes 22:55

2

Opens 11:30
Closes 18:50

3

Opens 13:00
Closes 1:30

4

Opens 9:30
Closes 17:15

5

Opens 12:15
Closes 19:30

6

Opens 8:30
Closes 15:20

7

Opens 6:45
Closes 14:25

8

Opens 8:00
Closes 16:35

9

Opens 12:00
Closes 23:45

e Each shop opens 25 minutes earlier and closes 10 minutes later. Write the new opening and closing times.

10 Katy is going to visit her granny in Newcastle.

She catches a train from Exeter at **8:30 a.m.**

The journey is due to take **7** hours **10** minutes, but the train is delayed by **20** minutes.

What time does Katy arrive in Newcastle?

Problems

11 Davinder's parents must feed his baby sister every **3** hours.

They feed her at **19:35.** What times in the night must they get up for the next three feeds?

12 An aeroplane flies from London to Amsterdam in Holland.

The plane leaves London at **18:30**. The flight takes **1** hour **45** minutes.

Holland is **1** hour ahead of Britain. What time is it in Holland when the aeroplane arrives?

Horizontal and vertical

Copy each shape.

Draw the:
horizontal lines in red,
vertical lines in blue,
other lines in yellow.

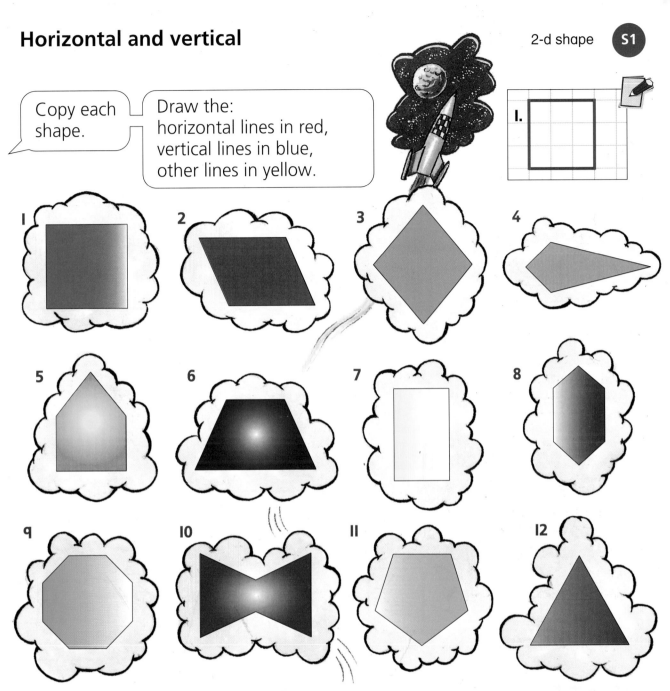

1.

1

2

3

4

5

6

7

8

9

10

11

12

@ Which shapes have parallel lines? Join the parallel lines.

Explore

Look at these rectangular grids.

Count how many horizontal and vertical lines you need to draw each grid.

Explore for different grids.

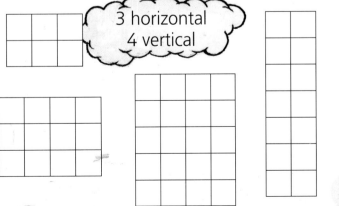

3 horizontal
4 vertical

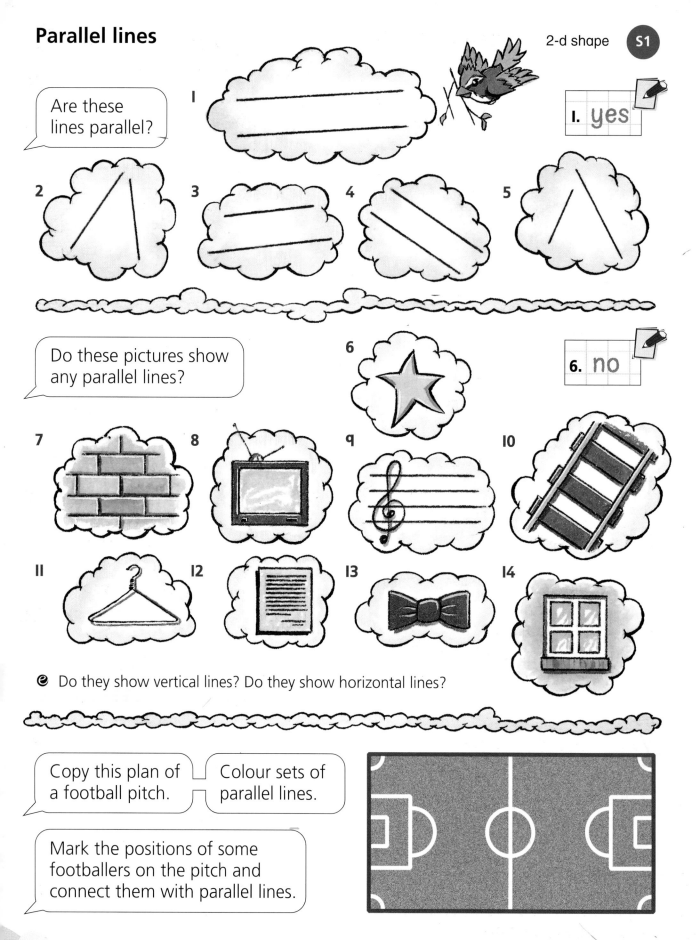

Are these lines parallel?

1

I. yes

Do these pictures show any parallel lines?

6

6. no

7   8   9   10

11   12   13   14

ℯ Do they show vertical lines? Do they show horizontal lines?

Copy this plan of a football pitch.

Colour sets of parallel lines.

Mark the positions of some footballers on the pitch and connect them with parallel lines.

ℯ Draw your own picture using parallel lines.

Parallel and perpendicular lines

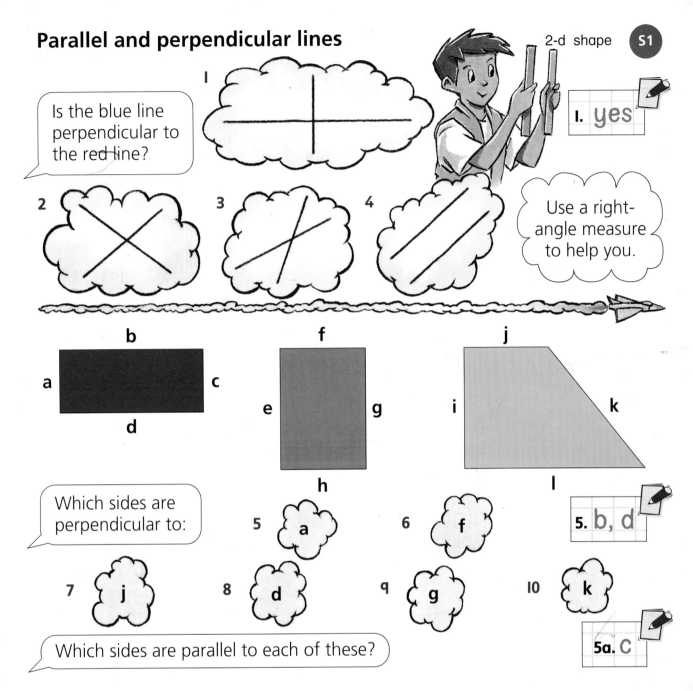

1 Is the blue line perpendicular to the red line?

Use a right-angle measure to help you.

2 **3** **4**

1. yes

Which sides are perpendicular to:

5 a **6** f

7 j **8** d **9** g **10** k

5. b, d

5a. c

Which sides are parallel to each of these?

e Which sides are vertical? Which are horizontal?

Explore

Z has parallel lines.

L has perpendicular lines.

H has parallel and perpendicular lines.

Explore parallel and perpendicular lines in other capital letters.

A no parallel lines
no perpendicular lines

B

C

27

Dimensions

Write '2-d' or '3-d' for the number of dimensions of each shape.

1

I. 3-d

2

3

4

5

6

7

8

9

10

e Write the number of faces for the 3-d shapes.

Draw 2-dimensional shapes with these properties.

11 I straight side
I curved side

II.

12 4 straight sides
I pair of parallel lines

13 3 straight sides
2 equal sides

14 6 equal straight sides

15 I curved side

16 4 straight sides
2 pairs of parallel lines

17 4 straight sides
all sides of different lengths

Regular and irregular polygons

Write the name of each shape.

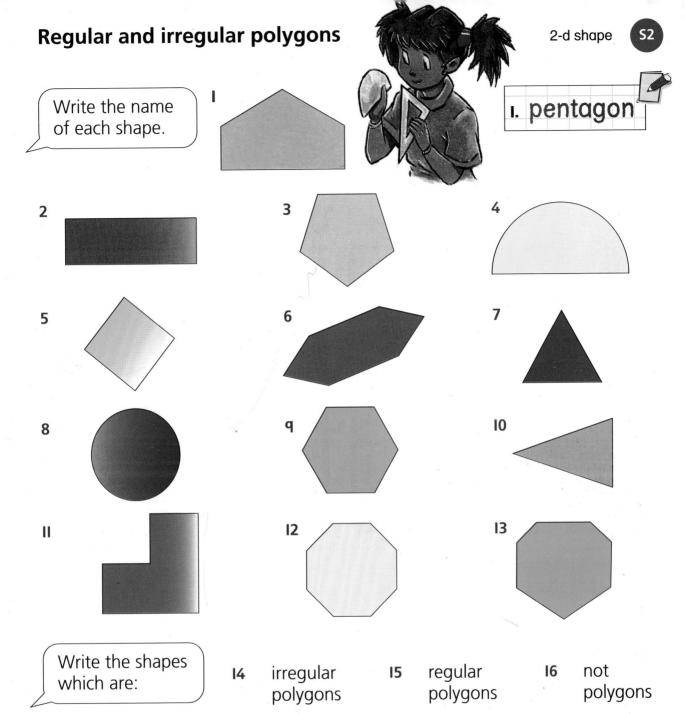

I

I. pentagon

2

3

4

5

6

7

8

9

10

11

12

13

Write the shapes which are:

14 irregular polygons

15 regular polygons

16 not polygons

Explore

Draw a regular and an irregular pentagon.

Draw the diagonals of each. How many diagonals do they have?

Explore the number of diagonals of other polygons.

Diagonals of a polygon

Write the name of each polygon.

1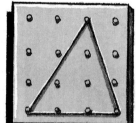

I. rectangle

2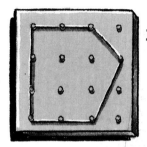

3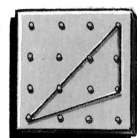

4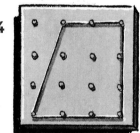

5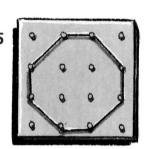

6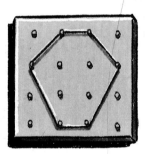

7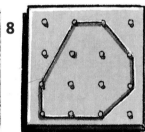

8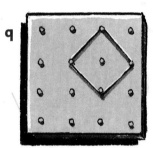

q

Copy each shape onto spotty paper.

Draw all the diagonals.

Write how many diagonals each has.

 Explore

Use a 3 × 3 geoboard.

Make polygons with different numbers of sides.

What is the largest number of sides a shape can have?

Draw the shapes on spotty paper.

Repeat using a 4 × 4 geoboard.

3 sides

Write 'isosceles' or 'equilateral' for each.

I. isosceles

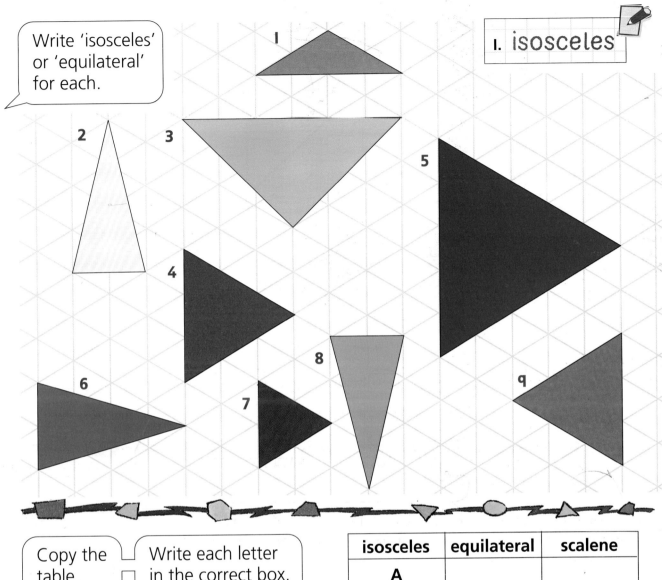

Copy the table.   Write each letter in the correct box.

isosceles	equilateral	scalene
A		

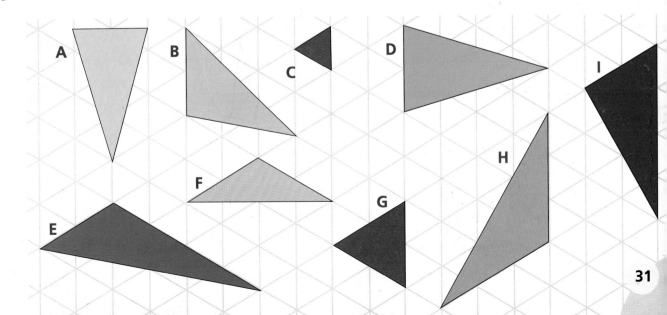

Right-angled triangles

Are these right-angled triangles?

I. yes

1 2 3 4

5 6

7

8 9 10

Copy each of these right-angled triangles onto squared paper.

Mark the right angle on each.

II.

11 12 13 14

15

17 16

18 19 20

Write 'scalene' or 'isosceles' for each.

11a. scalene

32

Triangles

Write the type of each triangle.

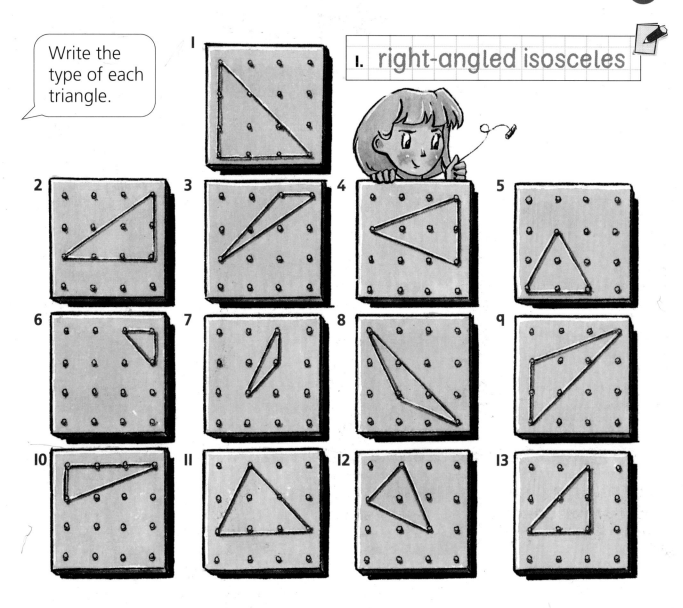

I. right-angled isosceles

Explore

Use squared paper.

Draw 4 right-angled isosceles triangles, all the same size.

Cut out the triangles and make shapes by joining them at equal side: Draw the shapes on squared paper.

How many different shapes can you make using 2, 3 and 4 triangles?

2 triangles

Reflective symmetry

Copy each shape. Draw any lines of symmetry.

I.

Use tracing paper or mirror, or cut out copies and fold them to help you.

1

2

3

4

5

6

7

8

Copy each shape. Draw any lines of symmetry.

q.

9

10

11

12

13

14

15

16

17

18

19

20

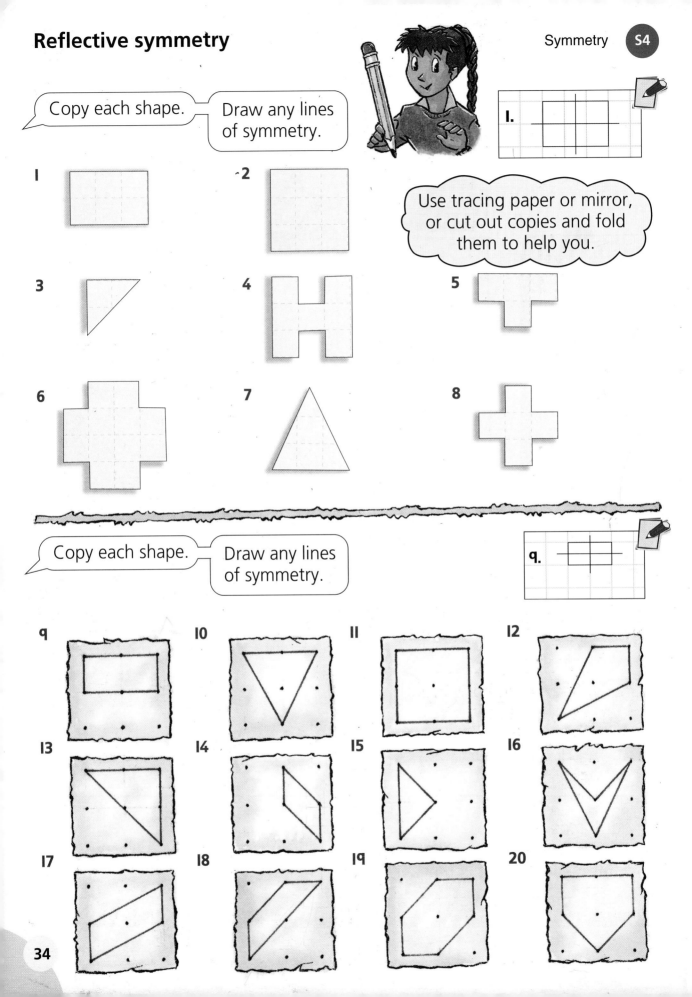

Reflective symmetry

Copy and complete the reflection for each shape.

I.

1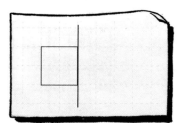

2

3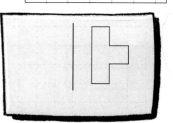

4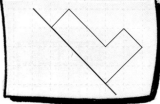

5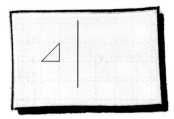

6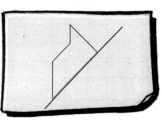

7

8

q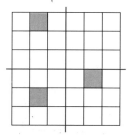

e Draw any other lines of symmetry for each.

Copy and complete the patterns.

10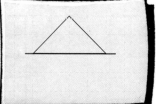

10.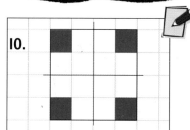

Draw reflections in both lines of symmetry for each.

11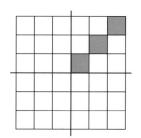

12

13

14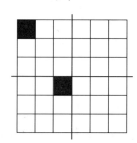

15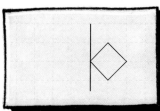

16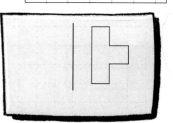

Reflective symmetry

Copy each pattern. Draw any lines of symmetry.

I.

1 **2** **3** **4**

5 **6** **7** **8**

9 **10** **11** **12**

e Draw some symmetrical patterns of your own.

Explore

Make 4 square tiles like this.

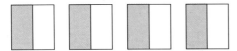

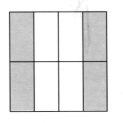

Arrange them to make a large square.

Investigate different patterns.

Record any patterns that have symmetry.

How many patterns can you make with 2 lines of symmetry? How many with more than 2?

Three-dimensional shapes

3-d shape **S5**

cone   pyramid   sphere   prism

cube   cuboid   cylinder

Write the name of each shape.

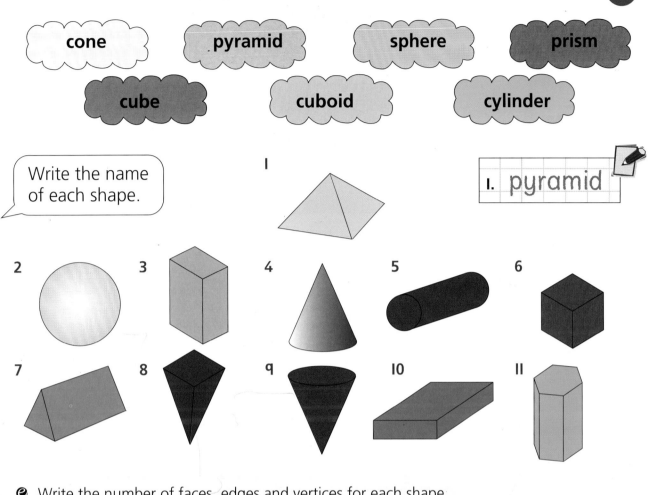

1

I. pyramid

2 3 4 5 6

7 8 9 10 11

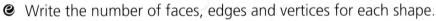

e Write the number of faces, edges and vertices for each shape.

Write the type of pyramid.

12. triangular-based pyramid

12 13 14 15

Write the type of prism.

16. pentagonal prism

16 17 18 19

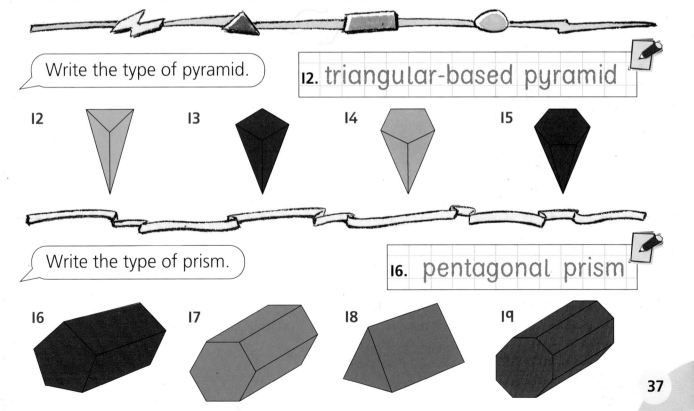

Faces, edges and vertices

Which shapes have these nets?

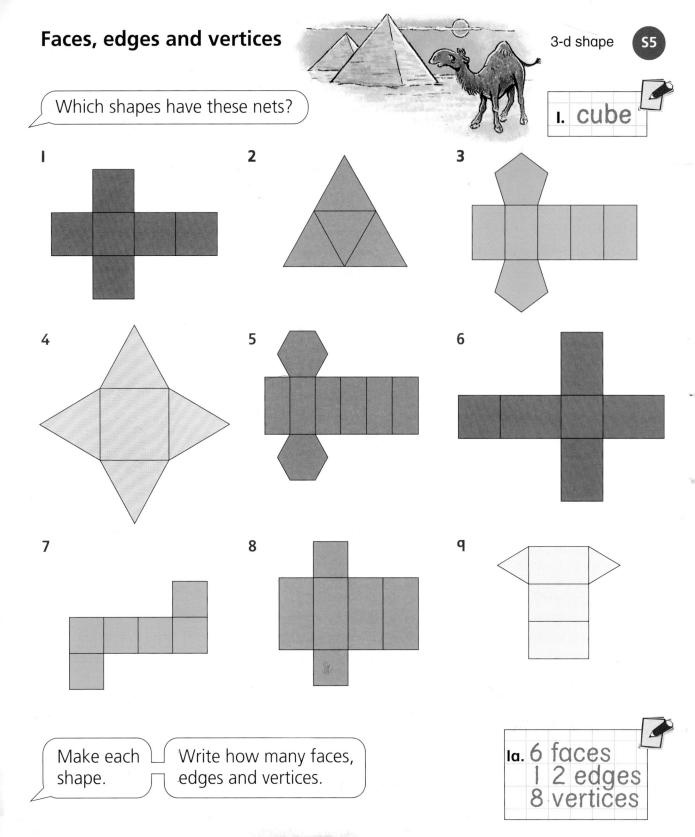

I. cube

1

2

3

4

5

6

7

8

q

Make each shape.

Write how many faces, edges and vertices.

Ia. 6 faces
12 edges
8 vertices

Describe the faces of each shape.

Ib. cube: 6 squares

Polyhedra

Are these polyhedra?

Write 'yes' or 'no'.

1. yes

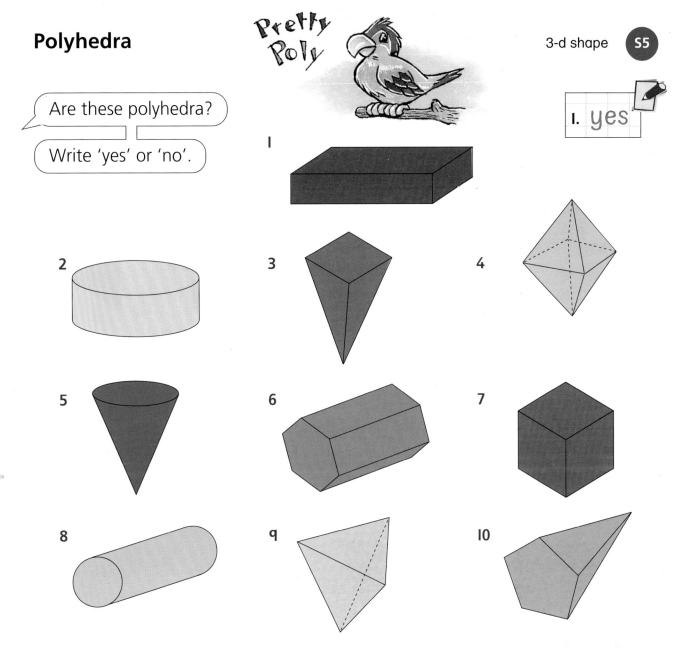

1

2

3

4

5

6

7

8

9

10

e Which are regular polyhedra? Write the name of each shape.

Explore

Use a set of solid shapes. Choose one shape.

Count how many faces and vertices. Add them.

Count how many edges. Take away this number.

Repeat for other shapes.

What do you notice?

Cube

6 faces
8 vertices

6 + 8 = 14

12 edges

14 − 12 = 2

One shape from each pair has been rotated 180°.

Write the pairs.

I. A and H

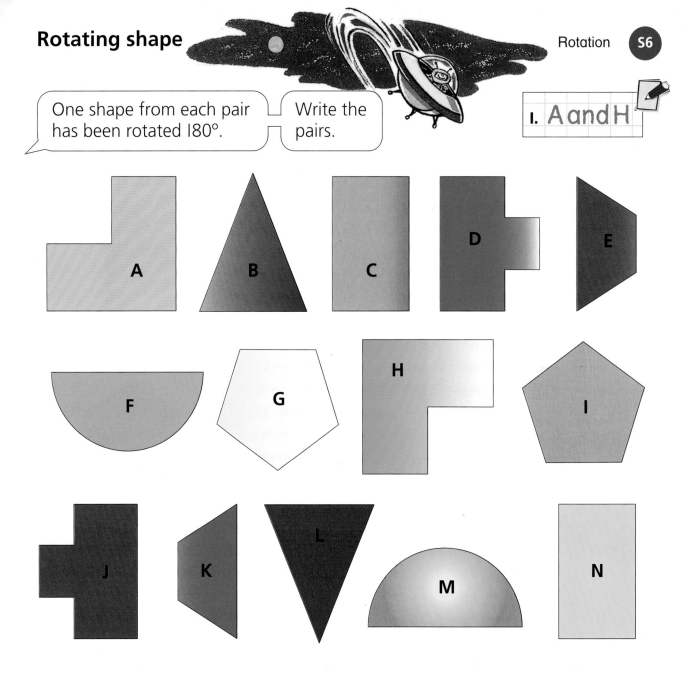

@ Draw the lines of symmetry for each shape.

Explore

Draw your own shape pairs, with one rotated 180°.

Use tracing paper to make a copy and turn it to test.

Rotating shapes and patterns

Copy each shape. Draw it rotated through 180°.

I.

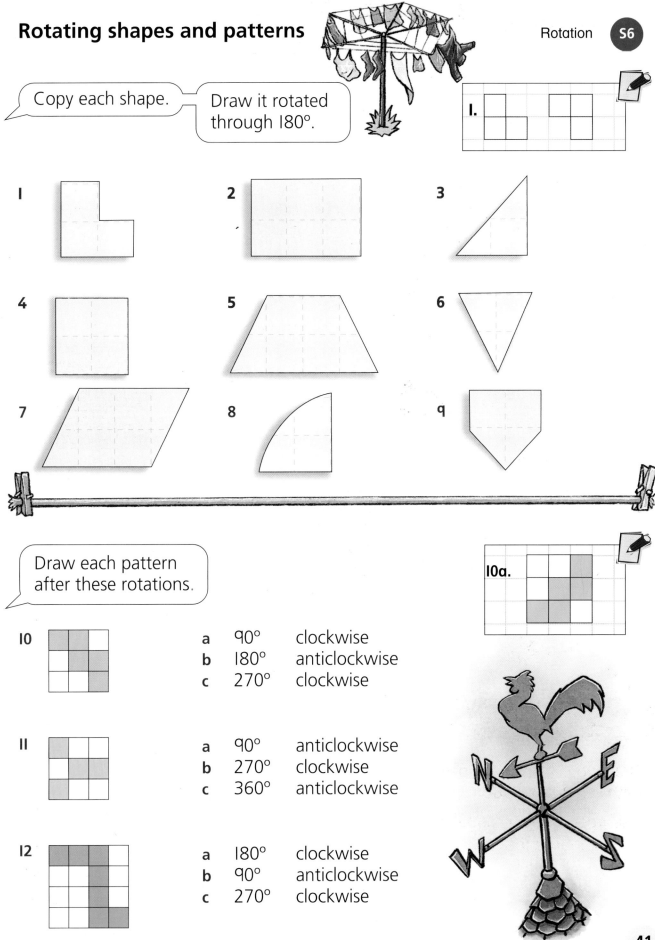

1

2

3

4

5

6

7

8

q

Draw each pattern after these rotations.

10a.

10

a 90° clockwise
b 180° anticlockwise
c 270° clockwise

11

a 90° anticlockwise
b 270° clockwise
c 360° anticlockwise

12

a 180° clockwise
b 90° anticlockwise
c 270° clockwise

41

Rotating shapes

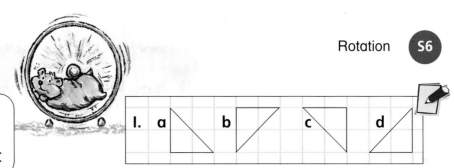

Draw the position of each shape after clockwise rotations of:

l. a b c d

a **90°**

b **180°**

c **270°**

d **360°**

l

2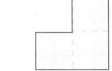

3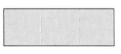

4

5

6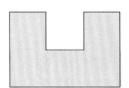

7

8

q

@ Draw the positions of the shape after anticlockwise rotations of 90°. What do you notice?

Explore

Draw a shape on squared paper.

Draw its position after clockwise rotations of 90°, 180°, 270° and 360°.

Repeat for other shapes.

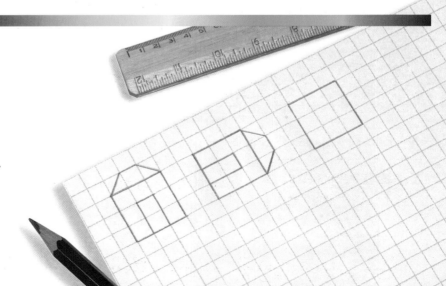

Coordinates

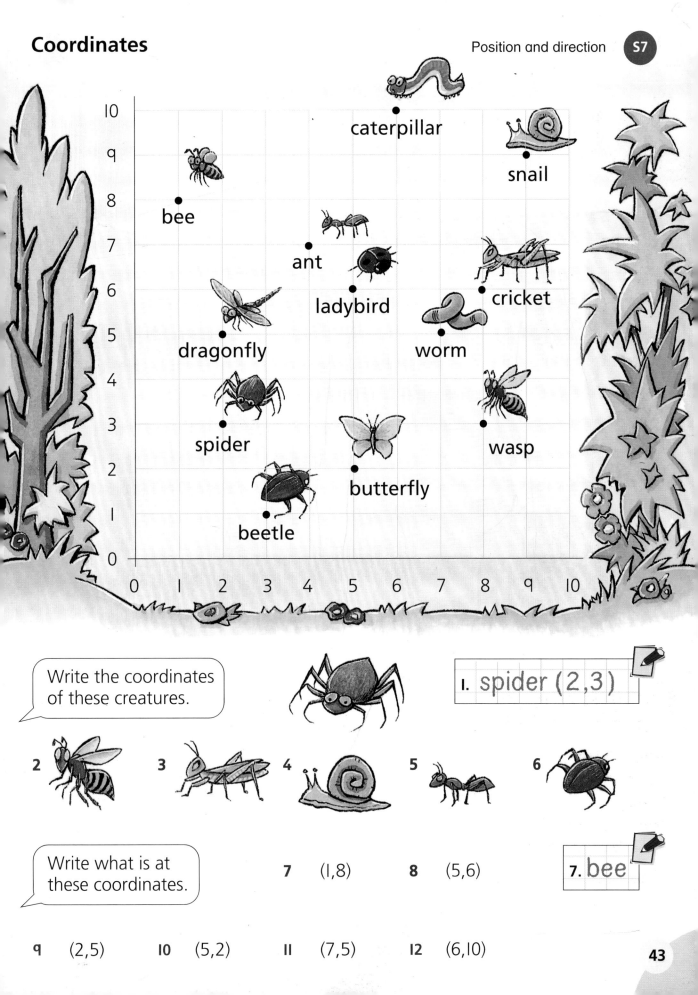

Write the coordinates of these creatures.

1. spider (2,3)

2.   3.   4.   5.   6.

Write what is at these coordinates.

7   (1,8)   8   (5,6)   7. bee

9   (2,5)   10   (5,2)   11   (7,5)   12   (6,10)

Coordinates

Draw a 10 × 10 grid. | Plot these points. | Join them in order. | Join the last point to the first point to complete the picture.

I (3,1)	**2** (4,2)	**3** (4,4)	**4** (0,4)	**5** (1,5)
6 (4,6)	**7** (4,8)	**8** (5,9)	**q** (6,8)	**10** (6,6)
II (9,5)	**12** (10,4)	**13** (6,4)	**14** (6,2)	**15** (7,1)

Write the coordinates of the points in the picture.

16. a=(1,1)

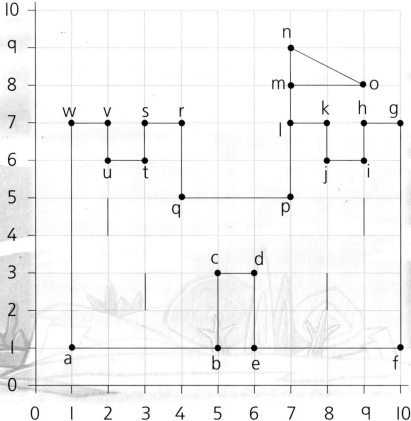

Explore

Write pairs of coordinates that add to make 10, e.g. (0,10), (1,9), (2,8)…

Plot them on a 10 × 10 grid. What do you notice?

Repeat for pairs that add to make 7, 11, 14,…

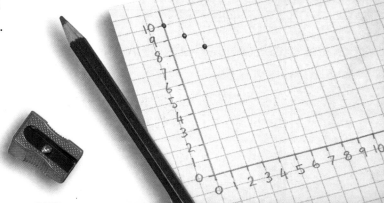

Coordinates

Write the explorer's new coordinates.

1. (5 , 3)

1 Start at (1,0). Go up 3 squares and right 4 squares.

2 Start at (1,2). Go right 2 squares and up 4 squares.

3 Start at (3,3). Go left 3 squares and down 2 squares.

4 Start at (6,4). Go down 3 squares and left 4 squares.

5 Start at (5,5). Go left 4 squares and up 2 squares.

6 Start at the origin. Go right 3 squares, up 2 squares and left 1 square.

7 Start at (4,6). Go down 2 squares, left 3 squares and up 1 square.

8 Start at (10,5). Go down 1 square, left 8 squares and down 3 squares.

9 Start at (6,0). Go up 8 squares, left 2 squares and down 2 squares.

e Write instructions for the explorer to get back to the origin each time.

Explore

The coordinates to make the capital letter F are:

(4,5), (2,5), (2,1), (2,3), (4,3)

Make other capital letters. Write the coordinates.

Can you write a message for a friend using coordinates for letters?

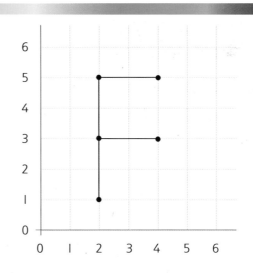

Degrees

Write how many right angles.

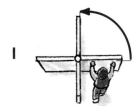

1. **I right angle**

 2

 3

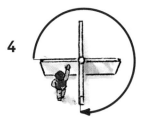 4

 5

 6

 7

 8

 q

Write how many degrees in each turn.

Ia. 9 0°

✎ Is each turn clockwise or anticlockwise?

Write how many right angles clockwise from:

Io. 2 right angles

10	N to S	**II**	E to N	**12**	W to N	**13**	N to NE
14	SW to NE	**15**	NW to E	**16**	NE to NW	**17**	SE to W
18	S to W	**19**	SW to W	**20**	SE to SW	**21**	N to SE

Write how many degrees in each turn.

Ioa. I 8 0°

46

Degrees

Write how many right angles turned by the hand on each stopwatch.

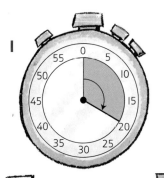

I

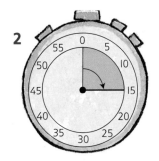 2

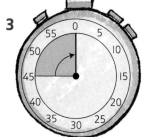 3

 4

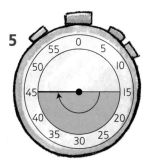 5

I. $1\frac{1}{3}$ right angles

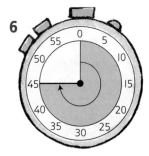 6

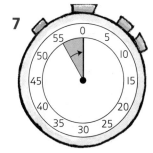 7

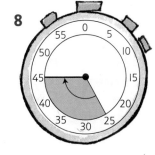 8

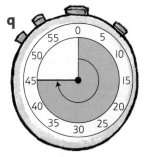 q

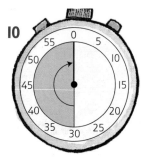 10

 II

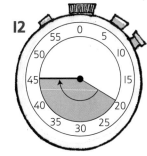 12

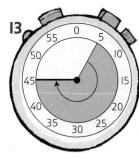 13

Write how many degrees in each turn.

Ia. $120°$

Write how many degrees turned by the stopwatch hand in:

14 5 seconds

I4. $30°$

15 30 seconds   16 15 seconds   17 50 seconds   18 25 seconds

19 40 seconds   20 60 seconds   21 35 seconds   22 10 seconds

47

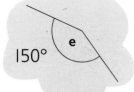
60° a

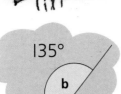
135°
b

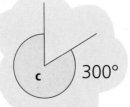
c 300°

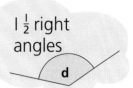
1½ right angles
d

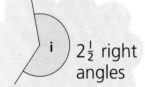
150° e

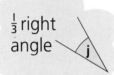
1 right angle
f

30° g

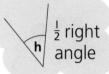
½ right angle
h

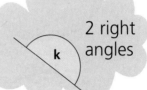
i 2½ right angles

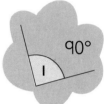
⅓ right angle
j

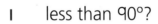
k 2 right angles

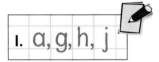
90°
l

Which of these angles are:

1   less than 90°?

1. a, g, h, j

2   between 90° and 180°?

3   the same?

4   more than 90°?

By how many degrees is:

5   **c** larger than **a**

5. 240°

6   **d** larger than **g**

7   **k** larger than **f**

8   **h** smaller than **e**

9   **k** larger than **b**

10   **a** larger than **g**

11   **b** smaller than **e**

Write all the angles in order, from smallest to largest.

30°, 45°,...

Degrees

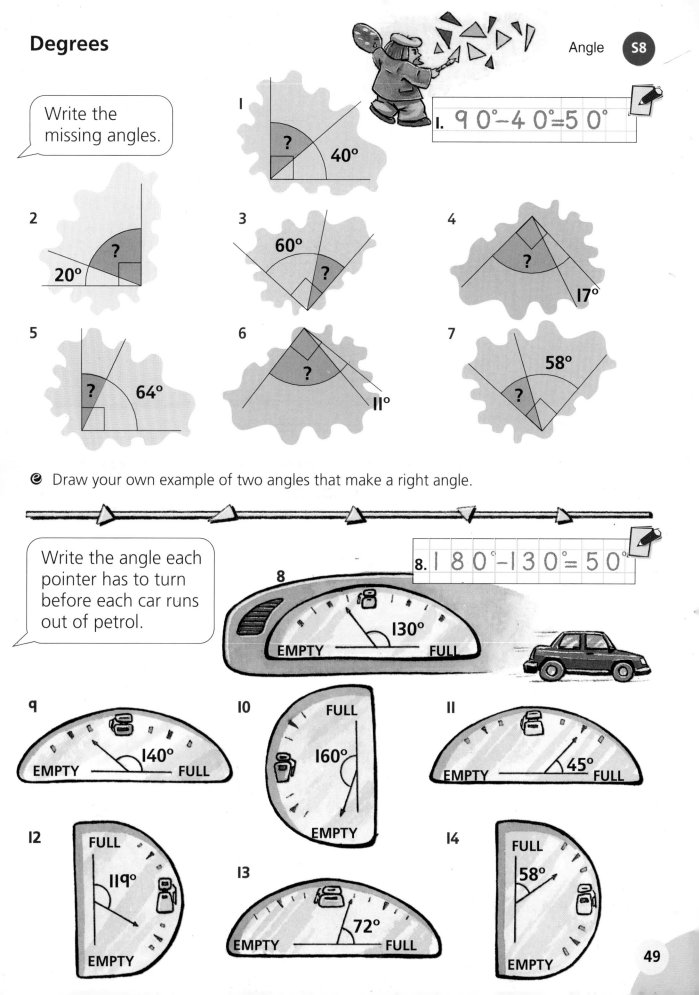

Angle **S8**

Write the missing angles.

1
? / 40°

I. 9 0°– 4 0°= 5 0°

2
20° / ?

3
60° / ?

4
? / 17°

5
? / 64°

6
? / 11°

7
58° / ?

e Draw your own example of two angles that make a right angle.

Write the angle each pointer has to turn before each car runs out of petrol.

8. 1 8 0°– 1 3 0°= 5 0°

8
130°
EMPTY — FULL

9
140°
EMPTY — FULL

10
FULL
160°
EMPTY

11
45°
EMPTY — FULL

12
FULL
119°
EMPTY

13
72°
EMPTY — FULL

14
FULL
58°
EMPTY

49

Measuring angles

Write how many degrees in each angle.

1. **6 0°**

1

2

3

4

5

6

Use a protractor to measure each of these angles.

A protractor

7. **5 0°**

8

7

9

12

11

10

Measuring angles

Estimate, then measure each angle.

A protractor

I. estimate: 3 8°
measure: 4 0°

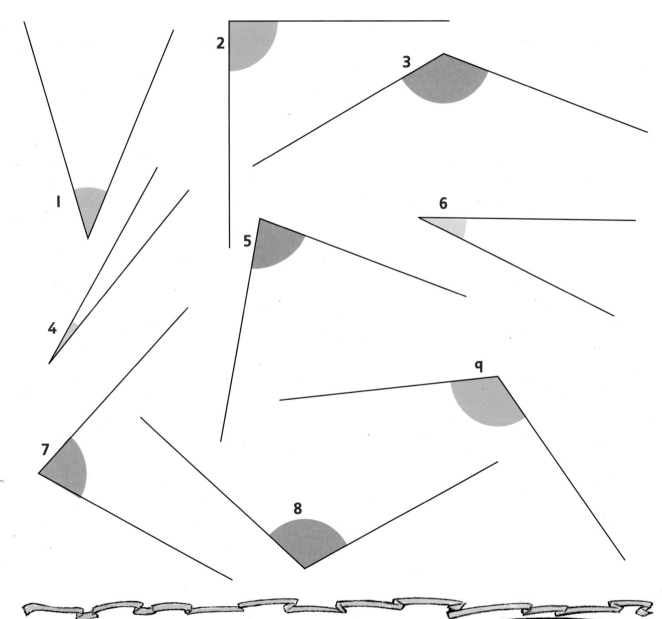

1

2

3

4

5

6

7

8

9

Draw each of these angles by estimating.

Measure each with a protractor to check.

A ruler
A protractor

| 10 | 50° | 11 | 90° | 12 | 20° | 13 | 70° |
| 14 | 120° | 15 | 45° | 16 | 180° | 17 | 135° |

Measuring angles

Measure the angles of each triangle.

A protractor

1. $a = 90°$

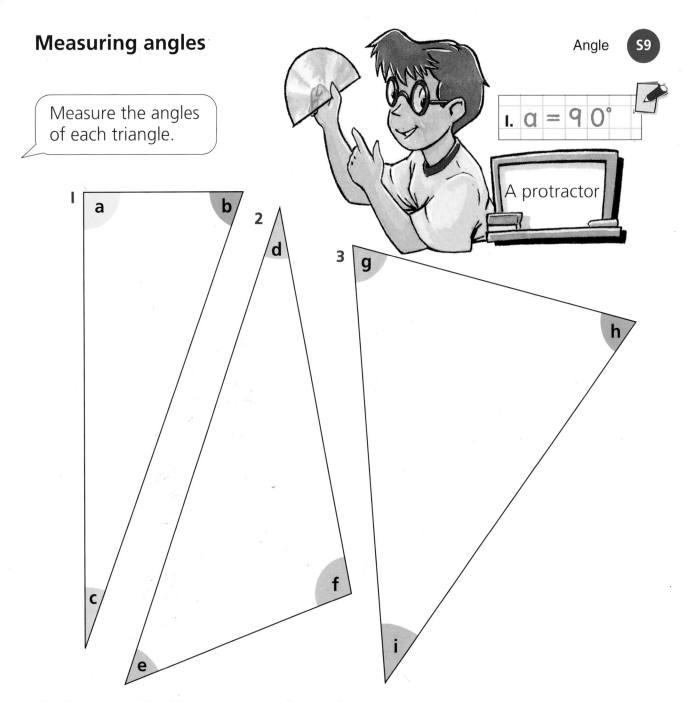

1 a b c

2 d e f

3 g h i

☻ Find the totals of the angles in each triangle.

Explore

Draw 5 large triangles. Measure the angles of each.

Find the total of the angles in each triangle. What do you notice?

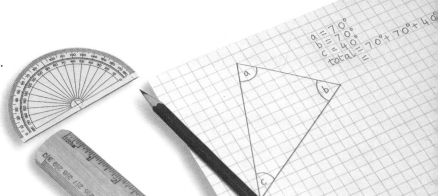

a = 70°
b = 70°
c = 40°
total = 70° + 70° + 40°

Types of angle

acute

obtuse

right angle

reflex

Describe the angle between each pair of boats.

1

1. acute

2

3

4

5

6

7

8

9

10

11

12

13

Describe each angle.

14 **30°**

14. 3 0°, acute

15 **90°**

16 **10°**

17 **120°**

18 **60°**

19 **115°**

20 **190°**

21 **100°**

22 **80°**

23 **240°**

24 **5°**

Types of angle

Describe each angle.

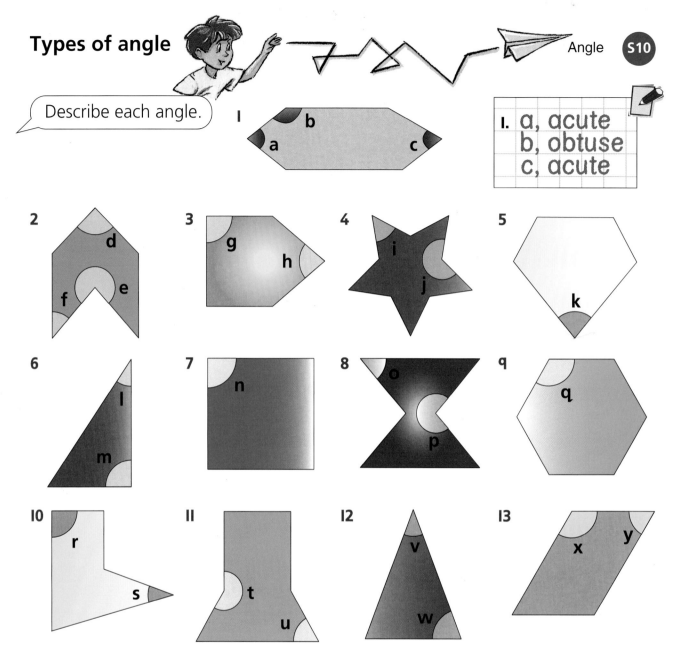

1. a, acute
b, obtuse
c, acute

Explore

Draw a hexagon with 1 reflex angle.

Draw a hexagon with 2 reflex angles.

Draw an octagon with 3 reflex angles.

Explore different polygons and the number of reflex angles they have.

Types of angle

Angle **S10**

> Describe the angle each car has turned.

 **I**

I. obtuse

2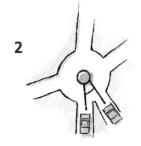

3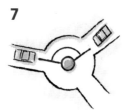

4

5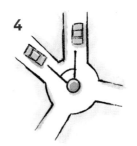

6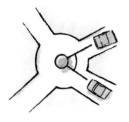

7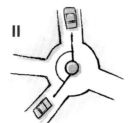

8

9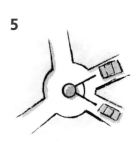

10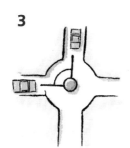

II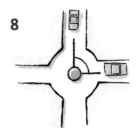

12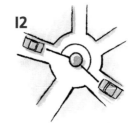

13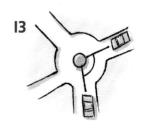

> Describe each clockwise angle of turn.

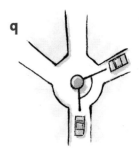

14. acute

14 N to NE	15 S to W	16 SW to NW
17 E to SE	18 NE to W	19 N to W
20 NW to SW	21 E to NE	22 S to NW

Types of angle

Write the type of angle.

Write 'acute', 'obtuse', or 'reflex'.

I. **obtuse**

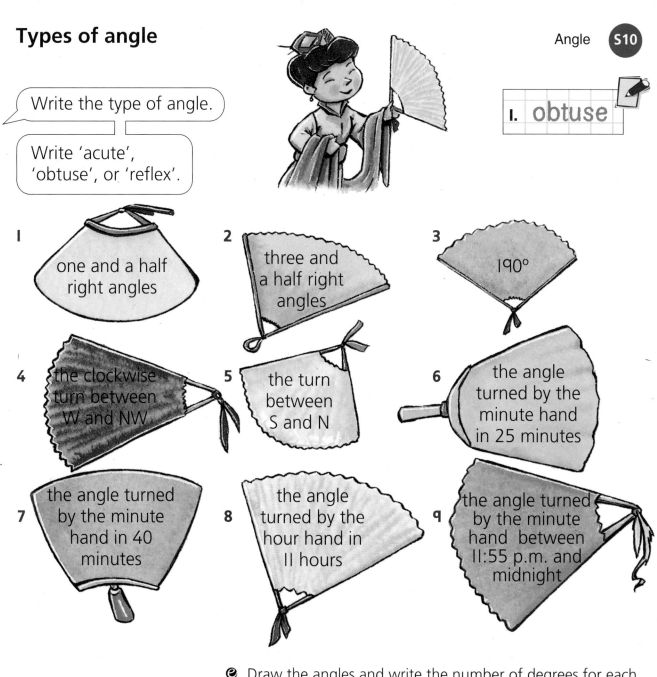

1 one and a half right angles

2 three and a half right angles

3 190°

4 the clockwise turn between W and NW

5 the turn between S and N

6 the angle turned by the minute hand in 25 minutes

7 the angle turned by the minute hand in 40 minutes

8 the angle turned by the hour hand in 11 hours

9 the angle turned by the minute hand between 11:55 p.m. and midnight

e Draw the angles and write the number of degrees for each.

Explore

Explore the angles of different quadrilaterals.

Is it possible to have a quadrilateral with:

- 4 acute angles?
- 2 reflex angles?
- 2 obtuse angles?

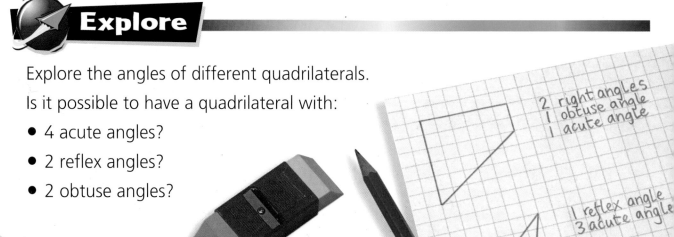

2 right angles
1 obtuse angle
1 acute angle

1 reflex angle
3 acute angle

Bar-line graphs

On Saturday 30 teams played one game of football each.

Number of teams (frequency)

Goals scored by 30 teams on Saturday

Goals scored

How many teams scored exactly:

1 3 goals?   **I.** 5 teams

2 0 goals?   **3** 5 goals?   **4** I goal?

5 2 goals?   **6** 4 goals?   **7** 6 goals?

How many goals were scored: **8** 3 times?   **8.** 3 goals

9 5 times?   **10** 7 times?   **II** more then 5 times?

12 4 times?   **13** 2 times?   **14** most often

How many teams scored: **15** more than 3 goals?   **15.** 5 teams

16 less than 2 goals?   **17** I or 2 goals?   **18** an odd number of goals?   **19** at least 3 goals?

57

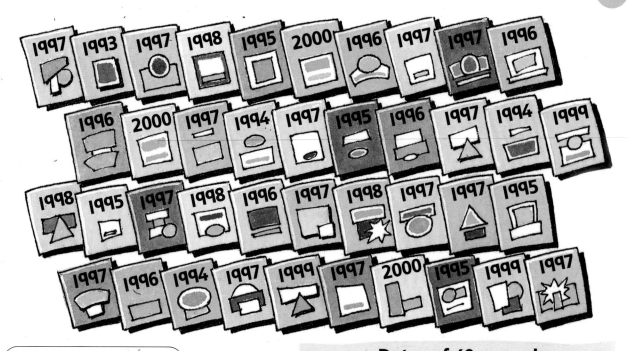

Copy and complete the bar-line graph to show the dates of these 40 annuals.

I. 6

How many annuals are from:

1 1996?

2 1993?

3 1998?

4 2000?

5 1997?

6 1999?

Dates of 40 annuals

Number of annuals (frequency)

20 —

10 —

0

93 94 95 96 97 98 99 00 → Year

Which year is the mode?

?

Explore

Deal 26 cards from a shuffled pack.

Draw a bar-line graph to show how many there are of each suit.

Bar-line graphs

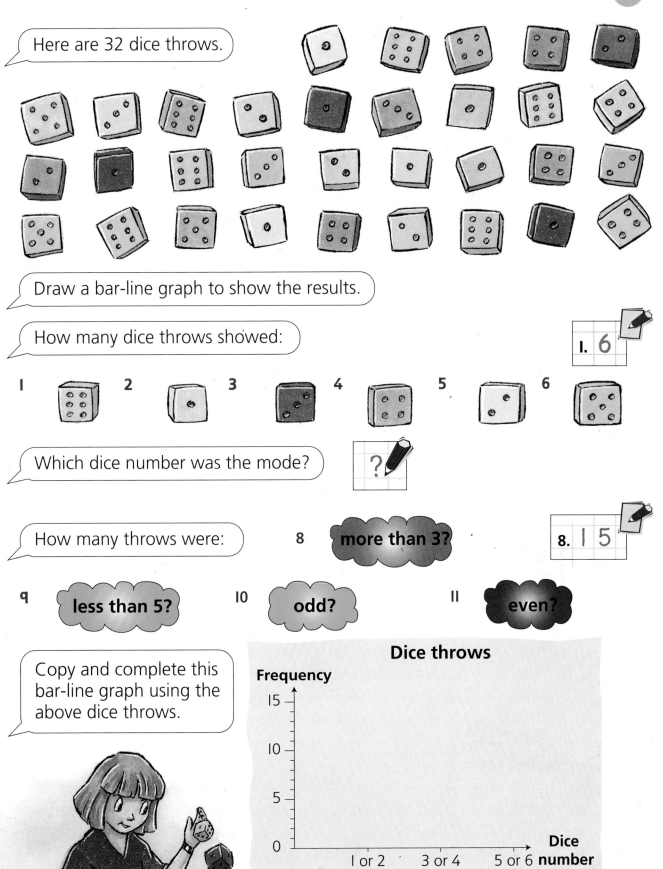

Here are 32 dice throws.

Draw a bar-line graph to show the results.

How many dice throws showed:

1. 2   3   4   5   6

1. 6

Which dice number was the mode?

?

How many throws were: 8   **more than 3?**

8. 15

9   **less than 5?**   10   **odd?**   11   **even?**

Copy and complete this bar-line graph using the above dice throws.

Dice throws

Frequency

15

10

5

0

1 or 2   3 or 4   5 or 6 **number**   **Dice**

Throw a dice 40 times and use your results to complete the bar-line graph.

Line graphs

The graph shows the changing temperature in a classroom.

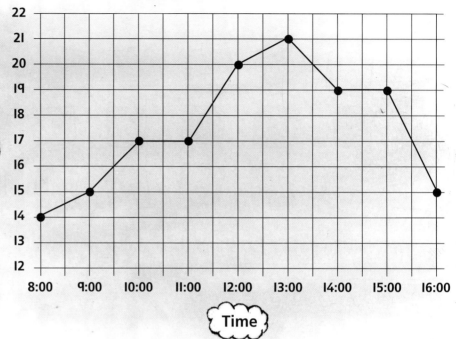

Temperature in the classroom

Temperature (°C)

Time

What is the temperature at:

1 9 o'clock?

1. 15℃

2 1 o'clock?	**3** 12 o'clock?	**4** 10 o'clock?	**5** 4 o'clock?
6 2 o'clock?	**7** half past 9?	**8** half past 3?	**9** half past 11?

At what time is the temperature:

10 15 °C? **11** 17 °C? **12** 20 °C?

13 16 °C? **14** 19 °C? **15** 18 °C? **16** at its warmest? **17** at its coldest?

Write a time when:

18 the room is getting warmer

19 the room is getting colder

What happens to the temperature between:

20 8:00 and 10:00? **21** 12:00 and 14:00?

22 13:00 and 16:00? **23** 10:00 and 11:00? **24** 11:00 and 13:00?

Line graphs

The graph shows the number of people watching television during one night.

Number of viewers (thousands)

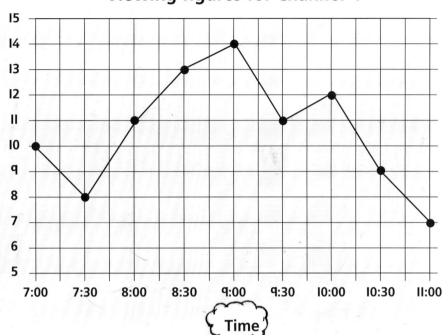

Viewing figures for Channel 9

Time

How many people are watching at:

1 8 o'clock?

1. 11,000

2 10 o'clock? **3** half past 7? **4** half past 8? **5** 7 o'clock?

6 half past 10? **7** half past 9? **8** 11 o'clock? **9** 9 o'clock?

At what time are these numbers of people watching?

10 10 000 **11** 14 000

12 7000 **13** 9000

14 8000 **15** 13 000

Write two times when the number of viewers:

16 is rising **17** is falling

What happens to the number of viewers between:

18 7:00 and 8:00? **19** 10:00 and 11:00?

20 8:00 and 9:00? **21** 9:00 and 10:00? **22** 9:30 and 10:30?

Line graphs

The table shows the height of a balloon.

Time	9:00	10:00	11:00	12:00	13:00	14:00	15:00	16:00	17:00
Height (m)	0	40	70	50	80	100	70	80	60

Draw a line graph to show the changing heights of the balloon.

Height (m)

Height of a balloon

100 —

50 —

0

9:00   10:00   11:00   12:00   13:00   14:00   15:00   16:00   17:00

Time

What is the height of the balloon at:

1 12 o'clock?   **1. 50 m**

2 3 o'clock?   **3** 10 o'clock?   **4** half past 12?   **5** half past 3?

At what times is the balloon at: **6** 80 metres?   **7** 40 metres?

8 60 metres?   **9** its highest?   **10** its lowest?

Write two times when the balloon is: **11** rising   **12** falling

What happens to the balloon between: **13** 9:00 and 11:00?   **14** 16:00 and 17:00?

15 12:00 and 14:00?   **16** 10:00 and 12:00?   **17** 14:00 and 16:00?

Likely and unlikely

| Impossible | Unlikely | Likely | Certain |

Write one label for each event.

I. unlikely

1 It will snow tomorrow.

2 I will use a computer today.

3 I will be famous one day.

4 I will fly next week.

5 I will see a dragon tomorrow.

6 I will be older next year.
 JUNE

7 I will sleep next week.

8 I will read a book next week.

9 I will eat tomorrow.

10 I will go to Mars one day.

11 It will be dark tonight.

12 I will play football this week.

13 I will be rich one day.

14 I will eat cheese this week.

15 I will watch TV tonight.

16 I will drive a car one day.

Write 2 impossible and 2 certain events.

Hello!

My dog will speak tomorrow – impossible.

Likely and unlikely

Impossible
I will see sheep fly tonight.

Unlikely
There will be a full moon tonight.

Likely
I will watch TV tonight.

Certain
I will sleep tonight.

Write your own 4 events for tomorrow.

Write your own 4 events for next week.

Explore

Work with a partner.

Write each of your 'likely' and 'unlikely' events from above on a card.

Place the cards in a line from least likely to most likely.

Agree with your partner where each card should go.

I will eat tuna tomorrow.

I will read a book next week.

It will snow tomorrow.

I will play football tomorrow.

I will walk my dog next week.